D0019064

BLOOD SUCKERS!

Deadly Mosquito Bites

John DiConsiglio

WARNING: Forget the buzz. With mosquitoes, it's all about the bite. These pests do more than ruin your picnic. They carry diseases that can make you sick—or even kill you. Read on—but beware their bite!

Franklin Watts
An Imprint of Scholastic Inc.
New York • Toronto • London • Auckland • Sydney
Mexico City • New Delhi • Hong Kong
Danbury, Connecticut

CONTENTS

TRUE or FALSE?

BIOHAZARD
BIOHAZARD

The mosquito is the deadliest creature on this page.

CALGARY PUBLIC LIBRARY

JUL   - 2010

TRUE!

Don't let its size fool you. The mosquito is one of the deadliest animals on earth. Tigers kill about 50 humans each year. Sharks kill even fewer. In 2005, sharks killed only four people.

Mosquitoes infect 500 million people around the world each year with malaria and other diseases. Their deadly bites kill more than 2 million people a year.

Book design Red Herring Design/NYC

Library of Congress Cataloging-in-Publication Data
DiConsiglio, John.
Blood suckers! : deadly mosquito bites / by John DiConsiglio.
p. cm. — 24/7 : sciences behind the scenes
Includes bibliographical references and index.
ISBN-13: 978-0-531-12070-5 (lib. bdg.)   978-0-531-17529-3 (pbk.)
ISBN-10: 0-531-12070-8 (lib. bdg.)   0-531-17529-4 (pbk.)
1. Mosquitoes as carriers of disease—Juvenile literature. I. Title.
RA640.D53 2007
614.4'323—dc22   2006021240

No part of this publication may be reproduced in whole or in part, or stored in a retrieval system, or transmitted in any form or by any means, electronic, mechanical, photocopying, recording, or otherwise, without written permission of the publisher. For information regarding permission, write to Scholastic Inc., 557 Broadway, New York, NY 10012.

© 2008 Scholastic Inc.
All rights reserved. Published by Franklin Watts, an imprint of Scholastic Inc.

Published simultaneously in Canada. Printed in China.

SCHOLASTIC, FRANKLIN WATTS, and associated logos are trademarks and/or registered trademarks of Scholastic Inc.
3 4 5 6 7 8 9 10 R 17 16 15 14 13 12 11 10 09

TRUE-LIFE CASE FILES!

These cases are 100% real. Find out how mosquito hunters try to zap deadly diseases.

Quinine is used to treat malaria in Los Angeles, CA.

15 Case #1:
Malaria and the Mother-to-Be

A pregnant woman is rushed to the hospital with malaria. Can doctors treat her disease without harming her unborn child?

23 Case #2:
Live from New York!

A mystery virus takes a bite out of the Big Apple. Can a bunch of dead birds help a doctor figure out what he's up against?

A mysterious disease is killing birds. Will it kill humans, too?

3 Case #3:

How did one scientist fight a disease-carrying mosquito? He moved in with it.

A scientist battles killer mosquitoes in Puerto Rico.

Are you itching for even more amazing info about mosquitoes?

Bzzz! A pesky mosquito lands on your arm and drinks some of your blood. It leaves behind an itchy bump. But if that's *all* it leaves behind, you should be happy!

MEDICAL 411

Every year, mosquitoes infect millions of people with deadly diseases. It's up to mosquito hunters— scientists and doctors— to stop them.

IN THIS SECTION:

- ▶ how mosquito hunters really talk;
- ▶ what you need to know about the diseases mosquitoes spread;
- ▶ people who work to stop deadly mosquitoes.

Buzz Words

Mosquito hunters have their own way of talking. Find out what their vocabulary means.

So many people have this disease that I'm afraid we have an **epidemic** on our hands. We need to call in an **epidemiologist** to help us.

epidemic
(ep-uh-DEM-ik) an outbreak of disease that spreads through a large number of people

epidemiologist
(ep-uh-DEE-mee-ahl-ul-jist) a person who studies how and why a disease spreads and figures out how to control it

We have no idea what this disease is and how it was **transmitted**. It's possible that it is a **mosquito-borne disease**.

mosquito-borne disease
(muh-SKEE-toh born duh-ZEEZ) a disease that is spread by a mosquito

transmitted
(tranz-MIT-ed) spread from one person or thing to another

We have the tests back. The patients have the **virus** that causes malaria. That's one of the most deadly diseases in the world.

virus
(VYE-ruhss) a tiny disease-causing organism that can reproduce and grow only when inside living cells

Believe it or not, these cases of malaria started with a tiny **parasite**. And that parasite was transmitted to humans by mosquitoes.

parasite
(PA-ruh-site) an animal or plant that gets its food by living on or inside another animal or plant

Say What?

Here's some other lingo a mosquito hunter might use on the job.

diagnosis
(dye-uhg-NOHS-sis) figuring out the cause of an illness based on tests and symptoms
*"The doctor will make her **diagnosis** once your test results are in."*

infectious disease
(in-FEK-shuhss duh-ZEEZ) an illness that spreads through water, food, air, body fluids, or carriers such as mosquitoes
*"Malaria is an **infectious disease** that is spread by mosquitoes."*

prognosis
(prog-NOH-sis) a prediction of how a disease will develop
*"My **prognosis** is that you will have no lasting effects from the disease."*

vector
(VEK-tor) something that carries a disease from one body to another
*"Mosquitoes are **vectors** for several diseases."*

Triple Threat

Here's a quick look at three diseases that are spread by mosquitoes.

MALARIA

Red blood cells infected with the organism that causes malaria

SYMPTOMS People get very tired and have chills, headaches, and muscle aches. Some have nausea, vomiting, and diarrhea. Malaria can also cause a yellowing of the skin and eyes.

HOW YOU GET IT Malaria was wiped out in the U.S. in the 1950s. But it still attacks much of the rest of the world. Malaria is caused by parasites in the mosquito's gut. The mosquito passes them to a person through its bite.

TREATMENT There's no **vaccine** for malaria. But there are many medications to treat it. If it is caught early, these drugs can work very well.

PROGNOSIS If you get treatment early, you have a good chance. If you wait too long, this disease can lead to kidney failure, **seizures**, **coma**, and even death.

[*Anopheles* mosquito]

WEST NILE VIRUS

SYMPTOMS About one out of five people who get the virus develop West Nile fever. That causes flu-like symptoms.

About one out of 100 has serious complications. These include **encephalitis** (swelling of the brain). Some suffer nerve damage and become **paralyzed**.

HOW YOU GET IT More than 130 species of birds carry this virus. When mosquitoes feed on infected birds, they pick up the virus. Then they give it to whatever they bite—birds, animals, or humans.

TREATMENT There is no cure or treatment for West Nile. In mild cases, the symptoms go away in about ten days. But some people feel sick for weeks. Use mosquito repellent!

PROGNOSIS The odds of getting West Nile are very slim. And the chances of dying from it are even slimmer.

Scientists are testing a West Nile vaccine. But it won't be ready for several years.

[*Culex* mosquito]

West Nile virus

DENGUE

HOW YOU GET IT Dengue is spread most often by the *Aedes aegypti* mosquito. The warm, wet regions of South America and Southeast Asia have serious dengue problems.

TREATMENT There is no treatment for dengue.

PROGNOSIS The worst symptoms last for about 10 days. A full recovery can take months. DHF can be fatal.

Dengue fever virus particles

[*Aedes aegypti* mosquito]

The Mosquito Hunters Team

Mosquito hunters work as a team to prevent the spread of disease.

ENTOMOLOGISTS
They work in the lab and the field, studying insects. They trap insects and study how they spread diseases.

EPIDEMIOLOGISTS
They work in areas that have been hit by diseases. They try to predict where a disease will strike next. They try to stop it from spreading.

PUBLIC HEALTH OFFICIALS
They are government officials who promote health. They run programs to try to stop the spread of diseases.

VIROLOGISTS
They study how viruses work, how they make people sick, and how they spread. They help develop treatments and vaccines.

ORNITHOLOGISTS
They work anywhere you find birds. They catch birds and study them. They find out how birds spread diseases.

FIELD BIOLOGISTS
They study how living things relate to their surroundings. Some count or collect mosquitoes. Others study birds that carry disease.

TRUE-LIFE CASE FILES!

24 hours a day, 7 days a week, 365 days a year, mosquito hunters are trying to treat and prevent mosquito-borne illnesses.

IN THIS SECTION:

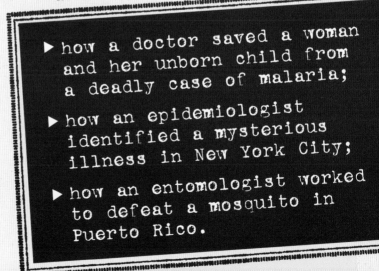

- ▶ how a doctor saved a woman and her unborn child from a deadly case of malaria;

- ▶ how an epidemiologist identified a mysterious illness in New York City;

- ▶ how an entomologist worked to defeat a mosquito in Puerto Rico.

These three case studies are true. However, names, places, and other details have been changed.

Mosquito FAQs

What's the buzz on those pesky pests?

QUESTION: Why do mosquitoes bite people?

ANSWER: Not all mosquitoes bite people. Just the females. They need the **protein** found in blood—human and animal—to reproduce. Every three to five days, a female pricks some flesh, drinks some blood, and lays her eggs.

Q: How do mosquitoes find humans?

A: Mosquitoes are attracted to carbon dioxide, the gas that we exhale. They follow the trail until they reach us. They can also detect body odors—like sweat. And body heat is also a powerful mosquito magnet.

Q: Why do mosquito bites itch?

A: The swelling and itch come from the insect's saliva.

Q: How does a mosquito transmit diseases?

A: A mosquito attacks you with a straw-like thing on its head called a **proboscis**. The proboscis enables the mosquito to suck out your blood. It also enables the mosquito to inject its saliva into your body. That's where disease comes from.

Q: How long do mosquitoes live?

A: Not long. Most mosquitoes live about two to three weeks. Some live as long as six months. And their eggs can survive for more than five years!

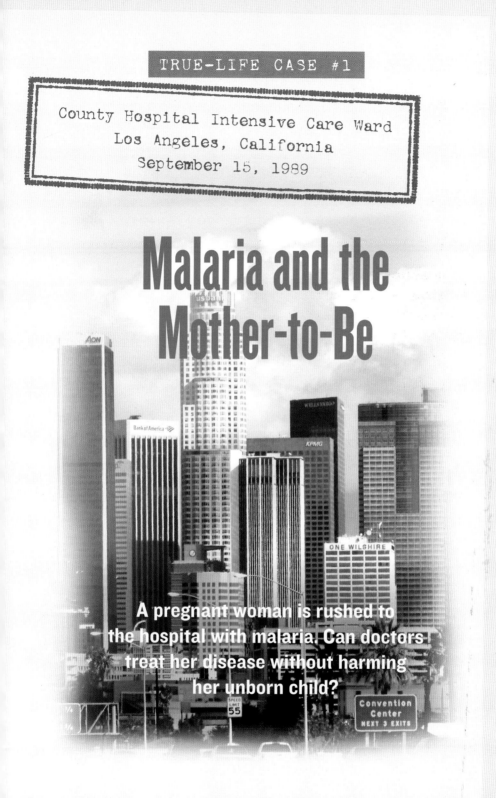

County Hospital Intensive Care Ward
Los Angeles, California
September 15, 1989

Malaria and the Mother-to-Be

A pregnant woman is rushed to the hospital with malaria. Can doctors treat her disease without harming her unborn child?

Parasites Found

A family visit suddenly becomes a matter of life and death.

Nadira Mulbah was in the intensive care ward of Los Angeles County Hospital. She had been vomiting for two days. The day before, she had woken up with fever and chills. "I think it's malaria," Mulbah told her husband, Togar. "This is exactly how I felt the other two times I had it."

The couple was visiting Togar's brother in Los Angeles, California. Being sick so far from home was upsetting, but that wasn't all that was worrying Mulbah. She was due to give birth to the couple's first child in a month.

A nurse took a sample of Mulbah's blood and sent it to the lab. There, a technician looked at a smear of her blood under a microscope. He spotted malaria parasites.

"With malaria, when you look at red blood cells, you can see ringed forms," explains Dr. Rekha Murthy. She is an epidemiologist, and she handled Mulbah's case.

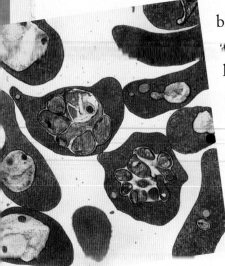

Patients with malaria have ringed forms inside their red blood cells. These are the parasites that cause malaria. Dr. Murthy explained, "We count the number of parasites per hundred cells. [Mulbah] had greater than 12 percent, which is in the dangerous range."

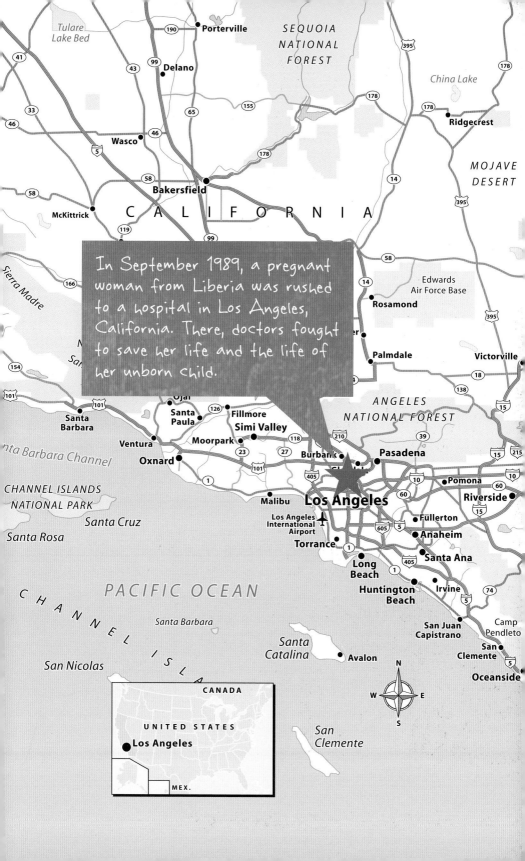

In September 1989, a pregnant woman from Liberia was rushed to a hospital in Los Angeles, California. There, doctors fought to save her life and the life of her unborn child.

WANTED: THE ANOPHELES MOSQUITO

Perhaps no insect in history has brought as much death and misery to the world as the *Anopheles* mosquito.

The *Anopheles* mosquito kills more than a million people every year. But it's not all the insect's fault. The mosquito picks up the malaria virus from a parasite, a tiny bug. The parasite grows in the mosquito's gut over the course of a week. Then it travels to the glands where the mosquito makes saliva.

A Tasty Treat

At dusk, the *Anopheles* starts searching for a blood meal. It will fly all night until it finds a tasty treat—a human. The parasites mix with the saliva and are injected into the human by the mosquito's bite.

There are about 400 species of *Anopheles*. About two dozen of them are vectors for malaria. The main malaria mosquito, *Anopheles gambiae*, thrives in high temperatures. The parasites in its gut need warmth to grow.

Malaria Lives

Around the 1950s, people tried to wipe out the *Anopheles* with **insecticides**. That would have brought malaria under control. But *Anopheles* is tough. Instead of dying out, it adapted to the chemicals in many insecticides. Today, malaria still survives in the hotter countries in Africa, Asia, South America, as well as Central America.

A Dangerous Situation

Doctors grow very concerned about the health of Mulbah and her unborn child.

"Even without the pregnancy to consider, this is a dangerous situation," Dr. Murthy told Mulbah. How could she and the other doctors save both Mulbah and her child?

First, an obstetrician, or baby doctor, ordered a special test that allows doctors to see inside Mulbah's belly. This test, called an ultrasound, helped them check on the baby's condition.

In the meantime, Mulbah had started to have contractions. Those cramps were a sign that she might have been ready to give birth.

And her condition was getting worse. It had been 12 hours since she had been admitted to the hospital. She had a headache. She was vomiting. Her vision was blurry.

Dr. Murthy, the obstetrician, and another doctor discussed how to save Mulbah and her baby. A full-term baby remains inside its mother's womb for 37 weeks. Often, babies are born earlier than expected. If they're at least 32 to 34 weeks old, they're usually okay. But Mulbah was only 31 weeks pregnant.

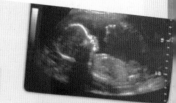

Ultrasound tests use sound waves to create an image of the baby inside of its mother. You can see that image on the screen above the technician's hand. Mulbah's obstetrician ordered an ultrasound to check on her baby.

Drastic Measures

Doctors replace some of Mulbah's blood. They also give her stronger medicine.

The doctors and nurses slowly fed new blood into Mulbah's veins, while taking away her diseased blood.

The doctors decided to take drastic measures to save Mulbah's life.

They called the blood bank. That's where blood that people donate is stored for surgery and other emergencies. Then they began blood **transfusions**. They slowly removed small portions of Mulbah's blood and replaced it with blood from the blood bank. They hoped this would lower the number of cells in Mulbah's blood that had malaria parasites.

Dr. Murthy also ordered **quinine** for Mulbah. That's a strong medicine that kills malaria parasites. At first, Dr. Murthy avoided giving Mulbah quinine because she feared it would harm the baby. Now, with Mulbah's condition getting worse, she had no choice.

Four hours later, the parasite count in Mulbah's blood had gone down. So Dr. Murthy continued the blood transfusions and the quinine.

Then there was another crisis. Mulbah's contractions started again. Another ultrasound test showed the baby's heartbeat was not steady. To save the baby, it had to be delivered. Now! Mulbah was rushed into surgery.

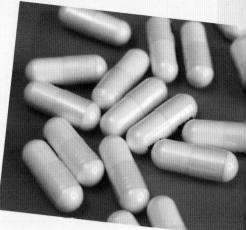

Quinine is a strong medicine that kills malaria parasites. Dr. Murthy gave it to Mulbah, even though she was concerned about its possible effect on Mulbah's baby.

Good News

The baby is born, and Mulbah's health improves.

Togar waited outside the operating room, frantic with worry. An hour passed. Finally, the obstetrician came out of the operating room. "You have a healthy baby boy," he said.

There was more good news. "Your wife's parasite count is down," the doctor went on. "She is definitely improving."

Mulbah took quinine for another three days. During that time, she stayed in her hospital bed, holding her new baby boy. Her husband stood beside them, beaming.

As for Dr. Murthy, she had a moment in the spotlight. She had treated Mulbah with quinine and blood transfusions. That had lowered Mulbah's fever and her parasite count—without harming the baby. This was groundbreaking. News of this new technique appeared in a medical journal—so other doctors could learn from Dr. Murthy. 24/7

Dr. Rekha Murthy explains what it takes to fight malaria and other infectious diseases.

24/7: Why did you decide to focus on epidemiology and infectious diseases?

DR. REKHA MURTHY: I got very interested because you have to know a lot about all of the body systems. And I was fascinated with the mysteries and detective work that ID [Infectious Disease] requires.

24/7: What are some of the challenges you've faced during your career?

MURTHY: I was starting in the field of ID at the beginning of the HIV epidemic. It was not yet understood. We didn't have treatments, and we saw young people dying.

More recently, we started seeing bacteria that were resistant to **antibiotics**. Suddenly, we had patients who were dying with infections for which we had no antibiotics. It was the same feeling of frustration and helplessness.

24/7: What type of personality is best suited for your job?

MURTHY: You have to be able to move quickly to find information, process it, and solve problems. In my field, there are these new infectious diseases such as SARS and bird flu. We have to get information as quickly as possible so we can be a resource for the other staff in the hospital.

In the first case, a doctor found a new way to treat a pregnant woman with an old disease. The doctor in the next case must figure out how to keep people safe from a mysterious new disease.

Live from New York!

A mysterious virus takes a bite out of the Big Apple. Can a bunch of dead birds help a doctor figure out what he's up against?

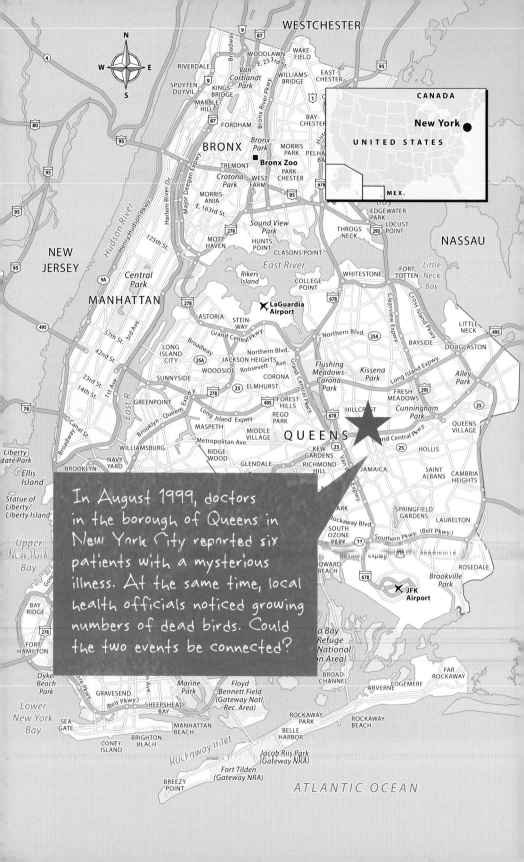

In August 1999, doctors in the borough of Queens in New York City reported six patients with a mysterious illness. At the same time, local health officials noticed growing numbers of dead birds. Could the two events be connected?

Virus Hunter

When people are sick—and doctors are stumped—epidemiologist Dr. Ned Hayes gets the call.

Dr. Hayes is an epidemiologist with the **CDC**. That's the U.S. agency that tracks and combats infectious diseases. It's his job to figure out why diseases occur—and how to prevent them.

But Dr. Hayes isn't interested in just any disease. The ones that really set his mind abuzz are diseases spread by insects. If a bug is making someone sick, it's up to Dr. Hayes to help catch it before whole communities— even whole countries—are infected.

Even Dr. Hayes wasn't prepared for the mystery insect disease that stung him and a team of scientists in the summer of 1999. It started like any ordinary case. A phone rang at the CDC with news of an insect disease to swat. But as Dr. Hayes and others investigated further, the new disease would turn out to be anything but normal.

Dr. Ned Hayes is an expert in highly contagious diseases. Whenever there's an outbreak, he gets a call.

DISEASE CENTRAL

For the past 60 years, the CDC have kept an eye on the health of the world.

"You may not know our name," a worker at the CDC says. "But you hear from us when an **outbreak** occurs and a quick response is needed."

The Centers for Disease Control and Prevention (CDC) is the U.S. government agency in charge of protecting public health. A key part of the agency's mission is to track and control contagious diseases.

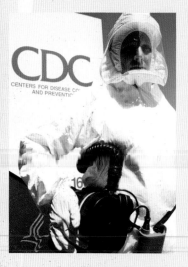

A worker from the CDC demonstrates a protective suit used during the study of the Ebola virus in 1995.

Mosquito Killers

The CDC started in 1946 in Atlanta, Georgia. At first, the organization focused mainly on the control of malaria—which meant killing mosquitoes. Scientists at the center organized a huge effort to spray an insecticide called DDT on more than six million homes. And by 1949, malaria was no longer a serious health problem in the U.S.

In 1958, scientists at the CDC made their first trip overseas. A team went to Southeast Asia to respond to an epidemic of smallpox and cholera.

Since then, the CDC has been active throughout the world, following infectious diseases such as smallpox, polio, tuberculosis, AIDS, and SARS.

Something Brand-New

Dr. Hayes knows a lot about diseases. But even he is surprised by this one.

Dr. Hayes and other scientists at the CDC were faced with a new mystery disease. Doctors from New York City were confused by unexplained cases of encephalitis. That's an **inflammation** of the brain. It's often fatal. One doctor saw two cases in a matter of days. And six cases were reported in the same neighborhood.

Encephalitis is caused by a virus. But these patients tested negative for the common viruses. That meant that somehow, they had caught a rare virus.

But how? The New York doctors suspected that the patients had gotten the virus from mosquitoes. After all, many of the patients lived near each other.

Doctors from the CDC requested the patients' blood samples from the New York City Health Department. These samples were tested. Results showed that the New Yorkers were indeed suffering from a mosquito-inflicted virus.

The patients had a disease called St. Louis encephalitis. That's a flu-like virus carried by mosquitoes in the *Culex* family. The mosquito becomes infected by feeding on sick birds.

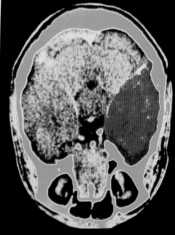

This CT scan of an adult's brain shows encephalitis on the right side of the brain (the red area). Encephalitis is an inflammation of the brain and can cause serious brain damage.

A number of birds in New York City died after being infected by mosquitoes. Was it possible that they had the same virus as the sick humans?

Then it passes the virus on to humans. The St. Louis virus can be ugly in humans, causing headaches and fevers.

The scientists were stunned. In the previous 40 years, there had been fewer than 5,000 cases of St. Louis encephalitis—and none in New York City. "Why the sudden outbreak?" they wondered.

The CDC scientists had a mystery on their hands. How did so many people come down with the same rare disease?

Before they could take a guess, the mystery deepened. About the same time that the mosquito virus showed up in New York, a doctor at New York City's Bronx Zoo called. Flamingos had died in the birdhouse. The **corpses** of other birds also littered the grounds. And each tested positive for a mosquito-borne virus.

Was this outbreak at the zoo related to the human outbreak?

The female *Culex* mosquito looks pretty harmless up close. But it carries many different diseases that can be harmful to humans, including St. Louis encephalitis and West Nile.

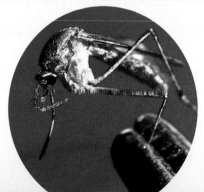

WANTED: THE CULEX MOSQUITO

The female *Culex* mosquito only lives a few weeks. But she sure makes the most of her time.

West Nile has been found in over 36 different kinds of mosquitoes. But the number one vector for the virus is the *Culex*.

There are actually two main types of *Culex* that carry West Nile. *Culex pipiens* is found on every continent except Antarctica. It breeds in polluted waters, such as city sewers and manholes. Its cousin, *Culex tarsalis* is found in great numbers in the western U.S. It breeds on irrigated farmland.

Blood Meals

The female *Culex* feeds on the blood of humans and animals. This gives her the protein she needs to produce several hundred eggs every few days.

Culex mosquitoes usually only live through the summer months. But they can hibernate through winter in warm, sheltered areas like garages, barns, or houses. And they're always back next summer—to lay more eggs and cause more trouble.

The Birds and the Mosquitoes

Scientists try to find the link between the dead birds and the sick humans.

Were the human and bird outbreaks related? The scientists were stumped. In some ways, it seemed like too much of a coincidence for both birds and humans to get sick with a mosquito-borne virus at the same time. But there were questions, too.

A researcher examines a dead bird. The West Nile cycle begins when mosquitoes bite infected birds. The mosquitoes can then transmit the virus when they bite other birds, animals, and people.

St. Louis encephalitis doesn't kill birds. Whatever was killing the Bronx Zoo birds had to be something different. To find out if the outbreaks were related, they had to figure out which virus had killed the birds at the zoo.

It was time to reach out for help. Vets from the Bronx Zoo sent the dead birds to the U.S. Department of Agriculture (USDA). Their lab can test for any mosquito-related disease.

A few days later, the birds tested positive for the West Nile virus. West Nile was first discovered in 1937 in Uganda, a country in Africa. It had never been seen in the U.S.

Suddenly, the mystery became clear. The blood tests on the humans had not been interpreted correctly. These patients didn't have St. Louis encephalitis. They had West Nile. The disease had probably hit the birds first. Mosquitoes had then fed on these birds and passed the disease on to humans. The disease was fatal to birds. But the humans had a chance.

WEST NILE MYTHS

Here are five common myths—and the whole truth—about the virus.

Myth #1: Kids have the greatest risk of developing West Nile.

Truth: Few kids get West Nile. People over 50 are at the highest risk of developing the most serious form of the disease.

Myth #2: You can get West Nile from sick birds.

Truth: People usually get West Nile from mosquitoes. There's no proof that you can get West Nile from handling infected birds. But you shouldn't do it—just in case.

Myth #3: West Nile is usually fatal.

Truth: West Nile is rarely fatal. In fact, many infected people never realize they are sick. CDC officials think that about 1.3 million Americans have gotten the disease. But from 1999 through 2006, only about 24,000 cases of West Nile were reported in the U.S. Fewer than 1,000 of those people died.

Myth #4: Mosquito repellents with the chemical **DEET** are not safe.

Truth: Experts say DEET is safe when used according to directions. Many people who want to avoid chemicals use oil of lemon eucalyptus.

Myth #5: After a few years, West Nile will die out.

Truth: Sorry. The only way to wipe out West Nile would be to kill every one of its natural hosts—birds—and every one of its vectors—mosquitoes. That's not going to happen. So the virus will probably be around for a long time.

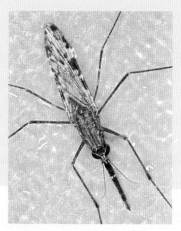

Mysteries Remain

Now Dr. Hayes knows what he is dealing with. But can it be stopped?

Dr. Hayes says we may never know for sure how West Nile suddenly arrived in the U.S. An infected mosquito may have hitched a ride on an airplane. Or a diseased bird could have ended up in New York. "All it would take is one mosquito and one bird to find each other for the whole transmission cycle to begin," he says.

An expert in a lab in Iowa extracts crow brain to test for the West Nile virus.

There were many questions to answer. The first was, How many New Yorkers were actually infected? To find out, Dr. Hayes had to gather more information. He organized a survey of people in New York City to find just how many people were sick with West Nile.

Surveyors went door-to-door, to hundreds of homes, asking important questions. Had anyone at the address gotten sick lately? What were their symptoms? Had they been near dead birds?

The next question was just as important. Could the team stop the virus from spreading? Dr. Hayes' survey estimated that more than 8,000 New Yorkers were infected with West Nile. Birds in Connecticut, New Jersey, and Maryland also tested positive, fueling fears that the virus was on the move.

WEST NILE ACTIVITY IN THE U.S.

Here's how the disease looked in 2006.

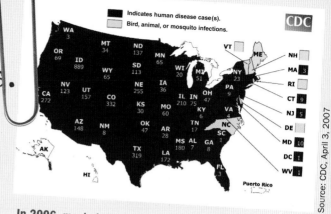

In 2006, most states in the U.S. experienced West Nile.

Source: CDC, April 3, 2007

"We sat back and realized the scope of what we had," Dr. Hayes says. "There was a new virus in our ecosystem."

Over the next few years, Dr. Hayes and the team of scientists watched West Nile spread across the country. The western Plains and the central U.S. appeared to be hardest hit. "Right now, it's **endemic** to the United States," Dr. Hayes says. That means the virus will always be here. Scientists believe it will flare up from summer to fall every year.

There's no cure for West Nile. Scientists are testing a vaccine. But it won't be ready for at least several years. Until then, Dr. Hayes and other scientists have worked with public health groups to teach Americans about West Nile. "Our best strategy is prevention," he says. "We can't kill the mosquito. We can't kill the virus. The only thing we can do is teach people how not to get sick." **24/7**

AVOIDING WEST NILE
Want to stay healthy? Here are five tips from Dr. Hayes.

1. Seal up your home. Make sure all your doors and windows have tight-fitting screens with no holes. Mosquitoes can squeeze through the tiniest openings!

2. Cover your body. Mosquitoes are most active between dusk and dawn. (That's nighttime.) If you go outside then, wear loose-fitting clothes that cover your legs and arms. Mosquitoes can bite through tight clothes.

3. Use mosquito repellent. During the summer and early fall, always smear some on—even if you're only going outside for a few minutes.

4. Look for standing water. That's the perfect breeding ground for mosquitoes. Empty water from flowerpots, pet dishes, and birdbaths. Clean out clogged rain gutters. Clean and add chlorine to swimming pools. Keep them covered when you're not using them.

5. Get involved! Ask about your community's mosquito control program. If your city doesn't have a program, tell officials that you want one. Now!

In this case, Dr. Hayes and his colleagues worked to identify a mysterious disease. In the next case, a scientist tries to protect people from a disease—and a mosquito—he knows all too well.

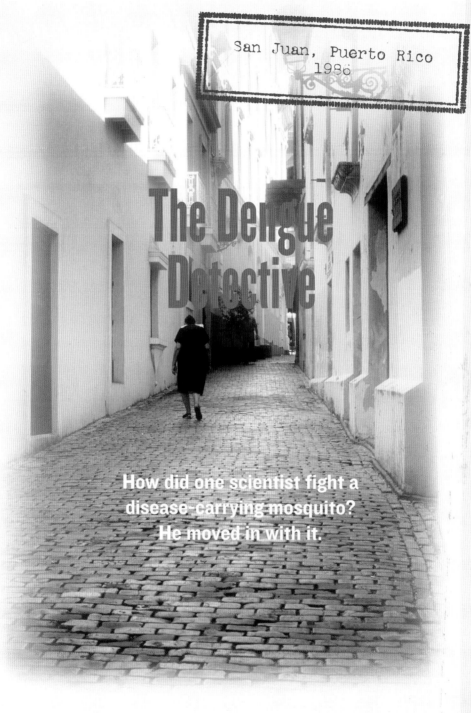

San Juan, Puerto Rico
1986

The Dengue Detective

How did one scientist fight a
disease-carrying mosquito?
He moved in with it.

Stalking the Enemy

Dr. Clark learns what he's up against in the fight to stop dengue.

There are many beautiful sights along the cobblestone streets of Old San Juan, Puerto Rico. But a trained scientific eye like Dr. Gary Clark's sees more than a tourist's. He sees 55-gallon (200-l) drums of water next to open windows. And water-filled paint cans on the edge of a sidewalk. And a child's pool in a front yard.

Dr. Clark is an entomologist. He studies insects. And to him, all of these were hiding spots for the *Aedes aegypti* mosquito. It's a tiny, dark mosquito with a sting no worse than that of any other insect. But few mosquitoes are as good at making people sick as *Aedes aegypti*.

For as many as 400 years, *Aedes aegypti* was famous for spreading a deadly virus called yellow fever. Today, a vaccine has wiped out yellow fever in many parts of the world.

But *Aedes aegypti* has moved on as a vector for another serious disease—dengue. Dengue rarely kills. But it can make people so sick that it takes weeks—or months—to recover. The symptoms include fevers, rashes, headaches, and terrible muscle and joint pain. In fact,

Dr. Gary Clark is an entomologist—an expert in insects. He spent 20 years in Puerto Rico, fighting dengue fever. Dr. Clark is now a research leader at the Mosquito and Fly Research Unit in Gainesville, Florida.

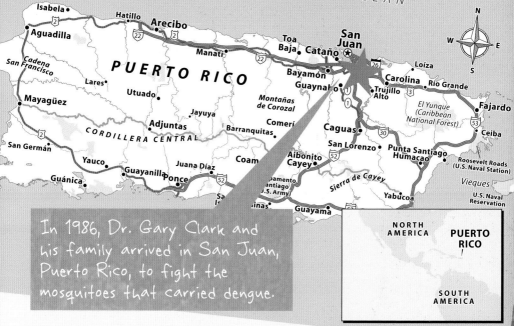

PUERTO RICO

In 1986, Dr. Gary Clark and his family arrived in San Juan, Puerto Rico, to fight the mosquitoes that carried dengue.

NORTH AMERICA   **PUERTO RICO**

SOUTH AMERICA

dengue's nickname is "break bone fever." As Dr. Clark puts it, "The pain is so intense, you feel like all your bones are breaking."

No one is sure how many people get dengue each year. According to the World Health Organization, it may be 20 million—or up to 100 million. In addition, each year about 20,000 people develop a fatal form of the disease called dengue hemorrhagic fever (DHF). Victims bleed uncontrollably from their noses, mouths, and gums. It strikes mostly children. There's no treatment—and no cure.

Until January 2006, Dr. Clark worked for the CDC. His job was to stop dengue dead in its tracks. And that meant figuring out how to wipe out the *Aedes aegypti* mosquitoes.

An *Aedes aegypti* mosquito feeding on a human host. This mosquito carries dengue, a disease that's so painful people refer to it as "break bone fever."

Part of the CDC's strategy was to attack the *Aedes aegypti* in its own backyard. The mosquito thrives in the hot, dry weather of the Caribbean Basin, Central and South America, Southeast Asia, and the South Pacific. So in 1985, Dr. Clark was sent to dengue's ground zero—San Juan, Puerto Rico.

WANTED: AEDES AEGYPTI

This tiny mosquito causes big trouble for people around the world.

Aedes aegypti doesn't look scary. It's only about 1/4-inch (6.4 mm) long, and its bite isn't fierce. Plus, it's skittish. It will quickly fly away with a brush of your hand.

Billions of Mosquitoes

So how did this little pest become such a menace? It's tough. Originally, the mosquito lived only in tropical jungles. But it learned to adapt to cities and suburbs.

It also reproduces a lot. Two mosquitoes can produce as many as 8 billion offspring in just a few months, says Dr. Clark.

Aedes aegypti breeds in water that collects in flower vases, old tires, and other everyday objects.

What's the best way to avoid being bitten by this bug? Experts say stay away from its breeding grounds and use insect repellent. But if *Aedes aegypti* wants to find you, it's hard to hide. It feeds in the daytime. So you're probably outdoors during its peak biting hours.

A female *Aedes aegypti*, after just filling up on human blood.

A More Dangerous Dengue

The virus rages on, becoming stronger and more deadly.

Dr. Clark arrived in San Juan, Puerto Rico, with his wife and three children. He was in charge of the CDC's Dengue Office. His goal was to help countries in the region stop the spread of the virus.

He told his wife that his fight against *Aedes aegypti* would probably last about four years. But it turned into a 20-year war. During that time, Dr. Clark and his wife even got the disease themselves.

Dr. Clark wasn't prepared for how much dengue had become a way of life in the area. "People just assumed that they were going to get this terrible disease at some point," he says. "They'd given up hope. They thought there was nothing they could do."

As many as 20,000 Puerto Ricans a year got dengue. But in the late 1980s, Dr. Clark saw an increase in DHF and fatal dengue cases. He was not sure why. It might have been the arrival of severe **strains** of dengue. Or humans may have introduced different dengue viruses when they flew in from other parts of the world.

The biggest concern was that DHF was becoming more common and taking more

An outdoor café in San Juan, Puerto Rico. Dr. Gary Clark moved to this city to help fight dengue, a mosquito-borne disease.

This is a sample of an *Aedes aegypti* mosquito's DNA. Scientists study the insect's makeup to better understand what they can use to fight it.

lives. It was not the "dengue of the past," Dr. Clark says. At first, dengue often looks a lot like the flu. But days after their fevers broke, patients, including many children, begin bleeding internally with DHF.

There was little Dr. Clark could do for the sick people. There was no vaccine and no treatment. If he was going to beat *Aedes aegypti*, he had to use another weapon. He had to make people understand that they could fight *Aedes aegypti*—and win.

THE YELLOW FEVER SCARE

The *Aedes aegypti* used to be known as the yellow fever mosquito.

At one time, yellow fever was a plague throughout the world.

In 1793, Philadelphia suffered the largest yellow fever epidemic in U.S. history. About 10 percent of the population—5,000 people—died. Thousands of people, including George Washington, fled the city in fear.

The outbreak ended when the cold weather froze the breeding grounds of the *Aedes aegypti*.

From 1793 to 1900, yellow fever caused more than 100,000 deaths in 135 separate U.S. epidemics. Scientists developed a yellow fever vaccine in the 1930s.

These days, yellow fever is almost never seen in the U.S. But it still kills about 30,000 unvaccinated people. Almost all of them live in Africa and South America.

Getting the Word Out

Dr. Clark teaches people the best way to defeat the deadly *Aedes aegypti*.

Health officials in Puerto Rico tried to kill the *Aedes aegypti*. They often drove through towns, spraying insecticides in the streets. But the mosquito spends most of its time indoors and won't fly into the poison clouds.

There was no way to change *Aedes aegypti*'s habits, Dr. Clark understood. Instead, he had to try something harder—changing people's habits.

Trucks like these sprayed insecticide to kill mosquitoes in Puerto Rico. But Dr. Clark knew that wouldn't be nearly enough to stop dengue.

With the help of local officials, Dr. Clark worked on educational programs, particularly for children. He worked with Head Start, the Boy Scouts, and children's museums. He taught people how and where mosquitoes breed and how they spread disease.

Dr. Clark's team included special troops: children. Cities such as San Juan held annual dengue fever parades. Kids marched through the streets dressed as doctors, nurses—even mosquitoes. They passed out flyers reminding people to turn over empty bottles and recycle used tires. The Head Start kids wore costumes made from insecticide cans to motivate people to join the fight against the dengue mosquito.

"It's all about getting the word out," Dr. Clark says. "We showed them that they didn't have to be mosquito food. They can fight back."

Dengue fever continues to be a serious issue in Puerto Rico—and throughout the world. In fact, the CDC calls it "the most important mosquito-borne viral disease affecting humans."

That's why Dr. Clark won't give up in his battle against the *Aedes aegypti*. "This insect has been around for maybe a million years," he says. "Every time mankind thinks it's licked, it comes up with a new way to spread a new disease to a new area of the world. People and mosquitoes are going to coexist for a long time. We have to get the upper hand." 24/7

Even Cub Scouts in Puerto Rico are helping to fight dengue. Here they are collecting water samples—to test for mosquito larvae.

MEDICAL
DOWNLOAD

You don't have to be a fly on the wall to find out more amazing stuff about mosquitoes. Just turn the page.

IN THIS SECTION:

- ▶ where mosquitoes have popped up in the past;

- ▶ news about mosquitoes and the diseases they spread;

- ▶ the tools people use to study mosquitoes;

- ▶ and whether being a mosquito hunter might be in your future!

400 B.C. Father Knows Best

A Greek doctor named Hippocrates (*right*) starts studying a mysterious disease. He keeps track of the symptoms. He also writes down the time of year people get sick and where they live. The disease eventually will be called malaria. And Hippocrates will be known as the Father of Medicine.

Key Dates in Mosquito

1879–1897 Malaria Milestoness

Two army doctors make strides in understanding malaria. Alphonse Laveran of France discovers the cause of the disease. He finds parasites in the blood of malaria patients. Then Ronald Ross (*above*) of Great Britain shows that malaria is spread by mosquitoes.

1937 West Nile Breaks Out

West Nile virus is detected for the first time when a woman in Uganda becomes sick. Soon, there are outbreaks of the virus in Israel, Egypt, South Africa, and parts of Europe and Asia.

1600s **A Bark with Bite**

Indians in Peru use the bark of a local tree to treat malaria. The tree is later named the Cinchona, after Spain's Countess of Chinchon. Legend has it that she was the first European treated with the bark (*below*). Chinchona bark contains quinine, which is still used to fight malaria today.

1818 **Fever Pitch**

An outbreak of dengue fever hits Peru (*above*). With 50,000 cases, it is the first reported dengue epidemic in history.

Hunting

Mosquitoes have been causing trouble for thousands of years.

1942 **It Kills Bugs Dead**

A chemical called DDT is invented and widely used (*below right*). At first it works well and kills large numbers of mosquitoes. But then some bugs learn how to adapt to it. And some nations, including the U.S., ban it after it proves harmful to wildlife.

1999 **Coming to America**

West Nile virus is reported in the U.S. for the first time when New York City has an outbreak. Over the next few years, it will appear all across the nation.

See Case #2.

In the News

Mosquitoes and the illnesses they spread are front-page news.

Experts Aim for Malaria Vaccine by 2025

BANGKOK, THAILAND—December 4, 2006

Experts from 35 countries have announced a plan to produce a vaccine against malaria by 2025. The vaccine would lower the number of people who get the disease by at least 80 percent. Today, 300 to 500 million people around the world get malaria each year. More than one million of them die.

Scientists are now testing more than 30 possible vaccines. The new plan will help them save time and money by sharing their research, says Dr. Melinda Moree. She is director of the group that came up with the plan. "Developing an effective malaria vaccine is an enormous challenge," she says, "but it is within reach."

Scientists hope to develop a malaria vaccine by 2025 to prevent outbreaks, such as the one shown to the left in the northeastern Indian city of Siliguri in 2005. During this outbreak, at least 15,000 people got the potentially fatal disease.

A volunteer in New Orleans places young mosquito fish in a pool flooded by Hurricane Katrina. The fish will help control the mosquito population.

Fish Fights Mosquitoes in New Orleans

NEW ORLEANS, LOUISIANA—April 2006

As New Orleans continues to recover from Hurricane Katrina, an unusual hero has come to town. *Gambusia affinis*, also called the western mosquito fish, is doing its part to keep the city safe.

Hurricane Katrina left more than 5,000 swimming pools full of dirty water. That makes them the perfect breeding ground for mosquitoes.

Mosquito fish eat the **larvae** that hatch from mosquito eggs. Each fish can eat about 100 larvae in a day. This month, volunteers started releasing 30 to 50 fish into each pool. They will stop the growth of new mosquitoes and keep away the diseases they carry.

Mosquito fish are now bred and kept in vector control centers around the country.

Meet the Mosquito

Take a close-up look at a mosquito and its life cycle.

ADULT FEMALE MOSQUITO

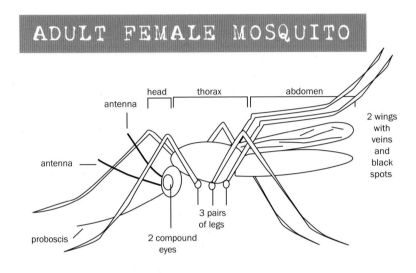

antenna The two antennae act like feelers and help the mosquito sense where it's going.

proboscis This looks like a tube and points down. The mosquito uses it like a straw to drink juices from a plant or blood from a human.

head The mosquito has two huge eyes. Each has many lenses that point in different directions.

thorax This is attached to the head and has scales that form patterns. The patterns help scientists tell what kind of mosquito it is.

abdomen This is attached to the thorax. It has eight pairs of air holes. The mosquito breathes through them.

wings The mosquito has two wings that are attached to the thorax.

legs The mosquito has six legs that are attached to the thorax. Each leg has a pair of tiny claws that help the mosquito balance.

THE LIFE CYCLE
OF THE MOSQUITO

ADULT

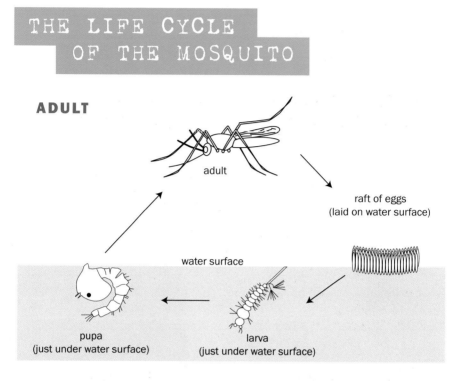

adult

raft of eggs
(laid on water surface)

water surface

pupa
(just under water surface)

larva
(just under water surface)

eggs Females lay 40 to 400 eggs in the water. They float together like a raft.

larvae Within a week, the eggs hatch into larvae. They shed their skin four times. Then they become **pupae**.

pupae These live near the surface of the water. After a few days, a pupa's covering splits and an adult mosquito comes out.

[Mosquito Fact]
When mosquitoes fly, their wings beat from 250 to 500 times each second.

Mosquito Repellent

Here's a look at the tools and equipment used by mosquito hunters.

repellent This is the most important item mosquito hunters use. They cover themselves—and their clothing—with it. There are only three types that the CDC has approved:
- products with the chemical DEET;
- products with the chemical Picaridin;
- oil of lemon eucalyptus.

petri dishes, microscope, glass vials Trapped mosquitoes are emptied onto petri dishes and counted under a microscope. They are sorted by species and placed in glass vials.

centrifuge Glass vials with mosquitoes are placed in a **centrifuge**. This machine swirls them around until they form a thick, watery mass. The liquid that rises to the top is tested for viruses.

mosquito traps, dry ice Scientists catch mosquitoes in canvas sacks with screen bottoms and battery-powered fans. The traps are hung overnight next to Styrofoam boxes filled with dry ice. The dry ice gives off carbon dioxide. That attracts the mosquitoes. Then the fan sucks them into the bags. The bags are gassed to knock out the mosquitoes. Any virus in their guts stays alive to be studied.

loose, light-colored clothing When weather permits, mosquito hunters wear long sleeves, long pants, and socks outdoors. They spray their clothes with repellents containing a chemical called permethrin. Warning: Permethrin is too powerful to spray directly on the skin. Scientists only use it on their clothing.

HIRED KILLERS

How do governments keep mosquitoes under control?

Many cities, states, and counties have mosquito control programs. Their purpose isn't to kill every single mosquito. It's to lower their population to a safe level. It's to prevent them from out-of-control breeding.

These programs often kill mosquitoes in their young stages—egg, larva, and pupa—before they become biting adults.

Officials keep track of the larval and adult mosquito populations. They track the path of disease-carrying mosquitoes. And often they spray insecticides, chemicals that kill adult mosquitoes. They also spray **larvicides**, chemicals that kill mosquito larvae.

HELP WANTED:
Mosquito Hunters

Interested in mosquito hunting? Here's more information about the field.

Sarah Wheeler is a staff research associate at the Center for Vectorborne Diseases at the University of California at Davis.

24/7: What does a field biologist do?

SARAH WHEELER: We spend a lot of time outdoors. I'm in the field, studying birds. I collect specimens and data that will later be used in the lab.

24/7: How do you catch birds?

WHEELER: If we're in a city, we'll set traps. But out in the field, we string these long nets between 9-foot (2.7 m) aluminum poles. They look sort of like volleyball nets. The birds get caught in them. We untangle them and take blood samples. We put bands around their legs so other scientists know they've been tested. Then we let them go.

24/7: What will the birds tell you?

WHEELER: When we test their blood, we'll see what birds are carrying West Nile and what their paths of **migration** are. That can tell us whether the birds got sick somewhere else — or picked up West Nile once they got here.

24/7: Where do you find the birds?

WHEELER: We're looking for places where birds and mosquitoes meet. The first place we went is a lake in California called the Salton Sea. It's a giant polluted salt lake right in the middle of a desert. It's muggy and buggy and it smells terrible. But I actually have a secret crush on the place.

24/7: Why is that?

WHEELER: All these different species meet there — the oddest-looking bugs and birds. Sometimes we catch birds that are weird mixtures. They'll have beaks of one bird and feathers of another. Seeing a bird like that makes my day.

24/7: What advice do you have for students who might want to become field biologists?

THE STATS: BIOLOGIST

DAY JOB: Biologists generally work in one of these four situations:
▶ private laboratories, such as those at pharmaceutical companies;
▶ universities, where they do research and teach;
▶ government laboratories, where they may work for groups like the CDC, the National Institutes of Health, or the National Science Foundation;
▶ independent research funded by grants.

MONEY: The average salary for a biologist is $69,908.

EDUCATION: Biologists can have many different levels of schooling:
▶ a bachelor's degree (4 years of college) is fine for some non-research jobs;
▶ a master's degree is fine for some jobs in applied research and product development;
▶ a PhD is usually necessary for independent research.

THE NUMBERS: The number of biological scientists grows every year. According to the Department of Labor, in 2004, there were 77,000 biologists working in the U.S.

WHEELER: You have to like being outside. Also, you should get your bachelor's degree in some form of biology. And you can get started right now. Wildlife and conservation groups would love your help!

DO YOU HAVE WHAT IT TAKES?

Take this totally unscientific quiz to find out if mosquito hunting might be a good career for you.

1 What's your feeling about bugs?
a) Neat! I can't get enough of the little critters.
b) They stay outside. I stay inside. Everyone's happy.
c) A bug? Where? Get it off me!

2 Can you handle lots of homework?
a) Bring it on.
b) It piles up, but I always finish it.
c) I think I left it in my locker. Or on the bus. Or under my bed.

3 Do you like science class?
a) It's my favorite. I could look into a microscope all day!
b) I'm doing well, but I'd rather be at lunch.
c) I wouldn't know. I'm usually asleep.

4 Do you like being outdoors?
a) Love it! The more I can be in nature, the better.
b) If the weather is nice, I'm there. But if it's too hot or cold, count me out.
c) Is there a place to plug in my PS3?

5 Are you easily grossed out?
a) The slimier the slug, the the more I like it
b) I can stomach it.
c) A paper cut? I'm going to faint.

1 2 3 4 5 6 7 8 9 10

YOUR SCORE
Give yourself 3 points for every "a" you chose. Give yourself 2 points for every "b" you chose. Give yourself 1 point for every "c" you chose.

If you got **13–15 points**, you're a born mosquito hunter.
If you got **10–12 points**, mosquito hunting might be a career option.
If you got **5–9 points**, this may not be the field for you.

HOW TO GET STARTED... NOW!

GET AN EDUCATION

▶ Read the newspaper. Keep up with news about the latest mosquito-borne diseases.

▶ Read anything else you find about mosquitoes. See the books and Web sites in the Resources section beginning on page 56.

▶ Take as many biology, zoology, botany, ecology, and chemistry courses as you can.

▶ Research colleges now. Start with their Web sites. Look for schools that have strong biology, zoology, and public health programs.

▶ Look into scholarships. Start with the BioQuip Undergraduate Scholarship and the Stanley Beck Fellowship, sponsored by The Entomological Foundation.

▶ Graduate from high school!

NETWORK!

Find out if your community has a mosquito-control program. If it does, contact the director. Ask if you can spend a day learning about what he or she does.

It's never too early to start working toward your goals.

GET AN INTERNSHIP

Get an internship with industries, universities, or government agencies that deal with insects. Or see if a local pest control company will take you on as an intern or summer employee.

LEARN ABOUT OTHER JOBS IN THE FIELD

▶ Doctors diagnose diseases from mosquitoes.

▶ Nurses help doctors treat them.

▶ Public health officials help people understand the dangers of mosquitoes. They also help prevent diseases from spreading.

▶ Inventors help design traps to catch insects.

▶ Ornithologists study birds, including those that carry the diseases spread by mosquitoes.

Resources

Looking for more information about forensic anthropology? Here are some resources you don't want to miss!

PROFESSIONAL ORGANIZATIONS

Centers for Disease Control and Prevention (CDC)
www.cdc.gov
1600 Clifton Rd
Atlanta, GA 30333
PHONE: 404-639-3311

The CDC is part of the U.S. Department of Health and Human Services. It was founded in 1946 to help control malaria. Since then it has headed up many public health efforts. It works to prevent and control infectious diseases. It also fights to prevent hazards in the workplace and health threats in the environment.

The Entomological Foundation
www.entfdn.org/index.php
2 Annapolis Road, Suite 210
Lanham, MD 20706
PHONE: 301-459-9082
FAX: 301-459-9084

The goal of this foundation is to educate young people in applying insect science to achieve a healthy environment. The group has a number of programs focusing on insect science. It also sponsors college scholarships for people interested in entomology.

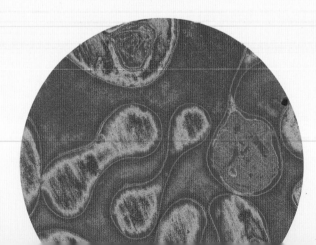

International Society for Environmental Epidemiology (ISEE)

www.iseepi.org

c/o JSI Research and
  Training Institute
44 Farnsworth Street
Boston, MA 02210
PHONE: 617-482-9485
E-MAIL: iseepi@jsi.org

The ISEE focuses on problems involving health and the environment. The group is open to scientists from around the world. They discuss, study, and educate people about issues such as infectious diseases and illnesses related to the environment.

National Institutes of Health (NIH)

www.nih.gov

9000 Rockville Pike
Bethesda, MD 20892
PHONE: 301-496-4000

NIH is the nation's medical research agency. It is part of the U.S. Department of Health and Human Services. It focuses on learning how to prevent and treat diseases.

WEB SITES

Health Canada
www.hc-sc.gc.ca/index_e.html

Health Canada is a department of the Canadian federal government. It focuses on helping Canadians achieve and maintain good health. The site has links to lots of information about diseases, research, and treatments.

Kids Health
www.kidshealth.org

KidsHealth is the largest site on the Web that focuses on the health of young people. It is divided into sites for kids, teens, and parents.

Mayo Clinic
www.mayoclinic.com

This site presents medical information from the 2,500 doctors and scientists who work for the Mayo Clinic in Rochester, Minnesota.

BOOKS ABOUT MOSQUITOES AND THE DISEASES THEY SPREAD

Abramovitz, Melissa. *West Nile Virus* (Diseases and Disorders). San Diego: Lucent Books, 2003.

Birch, Robin. *Mosquitoes Up Close* (Minibeasts Up Close). Chicago: Raintree, 2004.

Cefrey, Holly. *Yellow Fever.* New York: Rosen Publishing, 2001.

Day, Nancy. *Malaria, West Nile, and Other Mosquito-Borne Diseases* (Diseases and People). Berkeley Heights, N.J.: Enslow Publishers, 2001.

Lynette, Rachel. *Malaria* (Understanding Diseases and Disorders). San Diego: KidHaven Press, 2005.

Marcus, Bernard. *Malaria* (Deadly Diseases and Epidemics). Broomall, Pa.: Chelsea House Publishers, 2004.

McDonald, Mary Ann. *Mosquitoes* (Naturebooks). Mankato, Minn.: The Child's World, 2000.

Murphy, Jim. *An American Plague: The True and Terrifying Story of the Yellow Fever Epidemic of 1793.* New York: Clarion Books, 2003.

Skafianos, Jeffrey. *West Nile Virus* (Deadly Diseases and Epidemics). Broomall, Pa.: Chelsea House Publishers, 2005.

White, Katherine. *Dengue* (Epidemics). New York: Rosen Publishing, 2003.

The *Culex* mosquitoes, the carrier of the West Nile virus, are separated from other mosquitoes caught in traps throughout Arizona.

A

Aedes aegpti (AY-uh-dez uh-jip-TEE) *noun* a species of mosquito that transmits several diseases, including dengue and yellow fever

Anopheles (en-OHF-uh-leez) *noun* a species of mosquito that is known to transmit malaria

antibiotics (an-tuh-bye-OT-iks) *noun* medications given to patients to treat viruses

C

CDC (see-dee-SEE) *noun* a government agency in charge of protecting public health. It is short for the *Centers for Disease Control and Prevention.*

centrifuge (sen-truh-FYOOJ) *noun* a machine that separates materials of different densities. It is used in testing blood for viruses.

coma (KOH-muh) *noun* a state of deep unconsciousness

corpses (korps-ez) *noun* dead bodies

Culex (KYOO-lex) *noun* a species of mosquito most responsible for transmitting West Nile virus

D

DEET (deet) *noun* the active ingredient in commonly used insect repellents that are applied to the skin. Scientists have maintained that sprays containing DEET are effective against mosquitoes and safe if used as directed.

dengue (den-GEE) *noun* a virus spread by mosquitoes that causes fever, bad headaches, joint aches, and a rash. At least 20 million people—and as many as 100 million—contract it each year.

diagnosis (dye-uhg-NOHS-sis) *noun* the act of figuring out the cause of an illness based on tests and symptoms

E

encephalitis (en-seh-fah-LYE-tes) *noun* swelling of the brain caused by a virus. Severe cases of certain mosquito-transmitted diseases, like West Nile virus, can lead to fatal encephalitis.

endemic (en-DEM-ik) *adjective* describing a disease that will remain in a certain ecosystem; a disease that is here to stay

epidemic (ep-uh-DEM-ik) *noun* a widespread outbreak of disease that spreads within a specific region and/or country and affects a large number of people

epidemiologist (ep-uh-DEE-mee-ahl-uh-jist) *noun* a scientist who studies the patterns, causes, and control of disease in groups of people

I

infectious disease (in-FEK-shuhss duh-ZEEZ) *noun* an illness that spreads through water, food, air, body fluids, or carriers such as mosquitoes

inflammation (in-fluh-MAY-shuhn) *noun* redness, swelling, heat, and pain, usually caused by infection or injury

insecticides (in-SEK-tuh-sidez) *noun* chemicals used to kill insects

L

larvicides (LAR-vuh-sidez) *noun* chemicals used to kill insect larvae

larvae (LAR-vee) *noun* the immature, wingless life-forms that hatch from the eggs of many insects

M

malaria (ma-LAIR-ee-uh) *noun* a disease transmitted by the bite of a mosquito. It causes flu-like symptoms, including chills, fever, and sweating. Some forms can rapidly become deadly, leading to kidney failure, seizures, coma, and death.

migration (MYE-gra-shuhn) *noun* the act of moving from one place at one time of year to another place at another time of year

mosquito-borne disease (muh-SKEE-toh born duh-ZEEZ) *noun* an illness spread by a mosquito

O

outbreak (OUT-brake) *noun* the sudden spread of disease, in a short period of time and in a limited geographic location (like a neighborhood, community, school, or hospital)

P

paralyzed (PA-ruh-lized) *verb* made helpless or unable to move or function

parasite (PA-ruh-site) *noun* a microscopic plant or animal that lives in another organism

proboscis (prah-BAH-sis) *noun* the tube-like extension from a mosquito's head. The insect uses it like a straw to drink blood. The mosquito's saliva also drips through the proboscis, often transmitting diseases.

prognosis (prog-NOH-sis) *noun* a prediction of how a disease will develop and how it should be treated

protein (PROH-teen) *noun* a substance found in all living plant and animal cells

pupae (PYOO-pee) *noun* the "adolesent" life-forms of insects; they develop from the larvae

Q

quinine (KWY-nine) *noun* a drug to treat malaria. It comes from the bark of cinchona, a tree that grows in Peru.

S

seizures (SEE-zhurz) *noun* sudden attacks of illness or spasms

strains (straynz) *noun* specific versions or types of a bacteria or virus

symptoms (SIMP-tuhmz) *noun* health conditions that indicate you have an illness

T

transfusions (transs-FYOO-zhuhnz) *noun* injections of blood from one person into the body of someone else

transmitted (tranz-MIT-ed) *verb* spread from one person or thing to another

V

vaccine (VAK-seen) *noun* a substance that protects someone or something from the threat of illness

vector (VEK-tor) *noun* something that carries a disease from one body to another

virus (VYE-ruhss) *noun* a tiny disease-spreading organism that reproduces in the living cells of humans and animals

W

West Nile virus (west nile VYE-ruhss) *noun* a virus from a mosquito bite that causes weakness, fever, and sometimes swelling of the brain. Mosquitoes acquire the virus by biting infected birds. They can then pass it on to humans.

Index

Photo Credits: Photographs © 2008: age fotostock/Liane Cary: 15; Alamy Images: 5 right (Paul Crompton), 4 top, 10 bottom (Geoff du Feu), 39 (Robert Fried), 35 (Mark Lewis), 50 top (Niall McOnegal), 28 top (James Nesterwitz); AP Images: 51 top (Jim Bolt), 47 top (Bill Haber), 6 bottom (Patricia McDonnell), 32 (Buzz Orr/Iowa City Gazette); Centers for Disease Control and Prevention: 5 bottom, 37 bottom, 38 (James Gathany/Public Health Image Library), 1 bottom, 2, 31 (Public Health Image Library), 33; Corbis Images: 51 bottom (Richard A. Cooke), 44 top (Ed Eckstein), 41 (Thomas A. Ferrara), 42 (Karen Kasmauski), 26 (Shepard Sherbell); Courtesy of Dr. Gary Clark: 36; Courtesy of Edward B. Hayes: 25; Courtesy of Dr. Rekha Murthy: 22; Courtesy of Sarah Wheeler: 52; Getty Images: 19 (Chad Ehlers), cover (Hakan Hjort), 44 bottom, 45 bottom (Hulton Archive), 47 bottom (David McNew), 6 top, 45 top (Time Life Pictures), 28 bottom, 58 (Jeff Topping), 1 top left (Gary Vestal), 50 bottom; Image Source: 46 top; JupiterImages/Arend/Smith: 4 bottom, 8; Masterfile/Michael Goldman: 23; NEWSCOM/PRNewsFoto: 34; Peter Arnold Inc./David Scharf: 3; Photo Researchers, NY: 27 (AIRELLE-JOUBERT), 40 (Andy Crump, TDR, WHO), 11 bottom right (LSHTM), 16 (Dr. Gopal Murti), 45 center (SPL), 11 bottom left, 18, 64 (Sinclair Stammers), 11 top left (Dr. Linda Stannard, UCT), 11 top right (Larry West); Phototake: 10 top, 56 (Dr. Gary D. Gaugler), 5 top, 21 (Yoav Levy), 20 (Mendil/BSIP); Reuters/Rupak De Chowdhuri: 46 bottom; The Image Works/Spencer Ainsley: 30; VEER: 1 top right. Maps by David Lindroth, Inc.: 17, 24, 37

Ever since I was a little kid, I've had a problem with mosquitoes. It never seemed fair that I would get bitten and other people around me would not. I would play outside and come home itchy—while my brother had no problems. To me, it was just annoying. But now I know it could have been very dangerous to be bitten that many times.

With West Nile virus becoming a serious issue, protecting yourself against mosquitoes is even more important. I learned while writing this book that you can never be too cautious. After researching mosquitoes, I'll probably never go outside without wearing mosquito repellent!

For people who may be interested in mosquitoes or insects in general, one of the best places to see them is at the Smithsonian Museum of Natural History in Washington, D.C. Visitors can see all kinds of different insects and even talk to museum scientists and collectors about them.

CONTENT ADVISER: Mark S. Dworkin, MD, MPH & TM, Associate Professor, Division of Epidemiology and Biostatistics, University of Illinois at Chicago

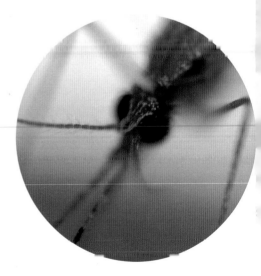